PROFESSIONAL SPORTS LEAGUES

MLB

BY MARTY GITLIN

CONTENT CONSULTANT
Stew Thornley
Sports Historian
Official Scorer, Minnesota Twins

Essential Library

An Imprint of Abdo Publishing | abdobooks.com

ABDOBOOKS.COM

Published by Abdo Publishing, a division of ABDO, PO Box 398166, Minneapolis, Minnesota 55439. Copyright © 2021 by Abdo Consulting Group, Inc. International copyrights reserved in all countries. No part of this book may be reproduced in any form without written permission from the publisher. Essential Library™ is a trademark and logo of Abdo Publishing.

Printed in the United States of America, North Mankato, Minnesota.
042020
092020

Cover Photos: Brian Rothmuller/Icon Sportswire/AP Images, foreground; Chris Bernacchi/AP Images, background
Interior Photos: Brandon Sloter/AP Images, 4, 14, 21 (background), 22 (background), 26–27 (background), 36, 46 (background), 48–49, 57 (background), 58, 68–69 (background), 78, 88, 90, 99 (background); Bettmann/Getty Images, 5; AP Images, 8, 19, 22 (foreground), 26–27 (foreground), 32, 37, 51, 61, 79; Jeff Roberson/AP Images, 11; Buyenlarge/Archive Photos/Getty Images, 15; Mark Rucker/Transcendental Graphics/Getty Images Sport/Getty Images, 17; Red Line Editorial, 21 (chart), 57 (chart), 99 (chart); Abe Fox/AP Images, 29; Cliff Schiappa/AP Images, 39; Eric Risberg/AP Images, 42; Gene J. Puskar/AP Images, 44; Ted S. Warren/AP Images, 46; Mike Janes/Four Seam Images/AP Images, 49; Zachary Lucy/Four Seam Images/AP Images, 56; Bill Kostroun/AP Images, 59; Charles Krupa/AP Images, 63; Mike Carlson/AP Images, 66; Photo Works/Shutterstock Images, 68–69 (foreground); Aaron Harris/AP Images, 72; David J. Phillip/AP Images, 75; Paul Newberry/AP Images, 83; Curtis Compton/Atlanta Journal-Constitution/AP Images, 85; Gary Stewart/AP Images, 88; Richard Cavalleri/Shutterstock Images, 91; Joyce Vincent/Shutterstock Images, 93; Ric Tapia/AP Images, 96

Editor: Arnold Ringstad
Series Designer: Dan Peluso

LIBRARY OF CONGRESS CONTROL NUMBER: 2019954180
PUBLISHER'S CATALOGING-IN-PUBLICATION DATA
Names: Gitlin, Marty, author.
Title: MLB / by Marty Gitlin
Description: Minneapolis, Minnesota : Abdo Publishing, 2021 | Series: Professional sports leagues | Includes online resources and index.
Identifiers: ISBN 9781532192067 (lib. bdg.) | ISBN 9781532179969 (ebook)
Subjects: LCSH: Major League Baseball (Organization)--Juvenile literature. | Baseball--Juvenile literature. | Professional sports franchises--Juvenile literature. | Sports--United States--History--Juvenile literature.
Classification: DDC 796.35764--dc23

CONTENTS

THE SHOT HEARD 'ROUND THE WORLD

Hitter Bobby Thomson and pitcher Ralph Branca were rival MLB stars in the early 1950s. ▶

The temperature was a sizzling 90 degrees Fahrenheit (32°C) in New York City on August 11, 1951. But that didn't compare to the Brooklyn Dodgers. They were red hot. They had won ten straight games to end July and had lost only a few games in the past few weeks. They owned a 69–35 record and a huge lead atop the National League (NL).

The Dodgers appeared destined to run away with the NL crown with only six weeks remaining in the regular season. But appearances can be deceiving. They suddenly cooled off. And their archrivals, the New York Giants, caught fire after stumbling through the first two-thirds of the season barely over .500. They won 16 in a row and ended the year on a long run of success. A thrilling pennant race concluded with the Giants and Dodgers tied at the top. A three-game series would determine the league champion.

Soon two of the biggest names in the league emerged in perhaps the greatest drama in baseball history. They were Dodgers pitcher Ralph Branca and Giants third baseman Bobby Thomson. Thomson set the tone for the series by smashing a two-run homer off Branca to win Game 1. Brooklyn bounced back to win the next day. The NL crown would be decided on October 3 at the legendary Polo Grounds, home of the Giants.

Brooklyn is a borough of New York City, so the two teams played only a few miles apart. The entire city was on edge. Fans had worked themselves up to a fever pitch. They awaited what many still consider the most anticipated battle in the history of the sport. When the Dodgers scored three runs in the eighth inning to take a 4–1 lead, the team once again seemed destined to snag the pennant.

Then it happened: one of the most memorable moments in baseball history. Super Dodgers pitcher Don Newcombe, who had been mowing down the Giants, began to falter. He gave up two singles, and after getting one out, Whitey Lockman hit a run-scoring double. One runner was on third, the tying run was on second base, and the potential winning run strode to the plate. It was Thomson. Brooklyn manager Charlie Dressen called to the bullpen for a relief pitcher. It was Branca. A feeling that lightning might strike twice washed over the sellout crowd. Giants fans hoped and Dodgers fans feared that Thomson would duplicate his Game 1 heroics against the right-hander.

WHAT'S ON TV?

Fans rarely watched baseball games involving teams outside their cities on television before the 1950s. That is when the *Game of the Week* was launched. One game was selected to be aired every Saturday during the baseball season until 1990, when the *Game of the Week* on NBC was canceled. CBS picked it up for three more years, but an increase in the number of games shown on cable ended the need for it.

Thomson's game-winning home run became legendary in baseball history.

Branca threw a fastball for strike one. Then he fired
another one, and Thomson took a mighty swing. The ball
shot like a laser into the left field stands for a game-winning
home run that would forever be known as "The Shot Heard
'Round the World." Brooklyn fans reacted with stunned
silence. Giants fans hugged each other and screamed with
delight. And radio announcer Russ Hodges blared out the
most famous call in baseball history: "The Giants win the

DID THE GIANTS CHEAT?

Did the 1951 Giants cheat to win the NL crown? Giants catcher Sal Yvars revealed in 1994 that his team placed spies in center field with a telescope to steal signs from opposing catchers. An electrician activated a buzzer in the bullpen—one buzz for a fastball and two for a curve. Yvars then signaled what was coming to Giants batters. He gave Thomson the fastball sign on the pitch that resulted in the game-winning home run in the playoff battle against the Dodgers. Thomson claimed his focus on Branca prevented him from looking for the sign.

pennant! The Giants win the pennant! The Giants win the pennant! . . . And they're going crazy!"[1]

BASEBALL'S GREAT MOMENTS AND MARKS

The one-on-one battle between hitter and pitcher is what makes baseball unique among major American sports. The spotlight on individuals at the plate, on the mound, and in the field has created many memorable moments. Some of the great moments have occurred in the World Series, sometimes known as the Fall Classic, which determines the ultimate champion of Major League Baseball (MLB).

There was Yankees slugger Babe Ruth growing his legend by slugging a home run in Game 3 in 1932. There was Giants super center fielder Willie Mays sprinting toward the center field wall and snagging a long drive at the Polo Grounds. The catch, made in Game 1 in 1954 to kill a Cleveland rally, is still cited as the greatest defensive play ever. There was also journeyman Yankees pitcher Don Larsen somehow throwing a perfect game in the 1956 World Series, and there was Pittsburgh Pirates star Bill Mazeroski smashing a homer to defeat the mighty Yankees in Game 7 in 1960. Another legendary moment came in 2011, when Saint Louis Cardinal David Freese hit a two-out, two-run triple to send Game 6 to extra innings. Freese then homered in the bottom of the eleventh inning to force Game 7, which the Cardinals went on to win.

The focus on individual performance allows for clearer statistical analysis in baseball than in other sports, and it also places a spotlight on records. The numbers compiled by players can be easily compared to those of their peers. The result is that many single-game, single-season, and career marks are hallowed in the annals of American sports. Baseball fans often know a record by the number alone. The number 755 is equated with the career home run mark set by Braves legend Hank Aaron. The number 56 is known as the consecutive-game hitting streak compiled by Yankees superstar Joe DiMaggio in 1941. The number 511 is recognized as the number of victories earned by pitcher Cy Young. But the history of the sport is more than singular moments and records. It is a journey that has lasted well over a century.

David Freese's postseason heroics in 2011 helped bring the Cardinals their eleventh World Series championship.

EVOLUTION OF THE GRAND OLD GAME

Though teams of professional players competed as early as 1869, some trace MLB back to the formation of the National League in 1876. The progression of the game has altered how, where, and even when it is played.

The basic setup became established in 1901 with the birth of the American League (AL), which, like the NL, featured eight teams. MLB has since consisted solely of the American League and the National League, aside from the brief existence of the Federal League from 1914 to 1915. And the champions of the NL and AL have battled for the World Series championship every year since 1903, with two exceptions. In 1904, the NL team refused to play the AL team. In 1994, a work stoppage that temporarily devastated the sport forced the cancellation of the Fall Classic.

One change began on May 24, 1935, at Crosley Field in Cincinnati. That was the date and site of the first night game in MLB. It was made possible by powerful outdoor lighting. Within 13 years every team but the Chicago Cubs—which finally installed lights at Wrigley Field in 1988—was playing night games. By the 1960s nearly every weekday game was played under the lights to accommodate schoolchildren and working people who could not attend games in the afternoon.

There were more teams playing those games by 1961. That year the MLB expansion era began. Both leagues added two franchises to give them ten by 1962. The addition of four more teams in 1969 further altered the setup. Both leagues were split into two divisions. The result was a playoff series in each league that created heightened regular-season excitement in more cities. Expansion continued into the 1990s. Each league had 15 teams in 2020, five of which earned playoff spots. Interleague play even allowed AL and NL teams to compete against each other in the regular season.

The focus in the modern era is on the future of the sport. It is on how to make baseball a better game for fans and players. But its rich history remains a beloved topic of discussion. That passion for baseball lore has not changed for more than a century.

COMINGS AND GOINGS

Expansion has not been the only method of bringing MLB to new cities in the modern era. Some franchises have simply moved from one city to another. The Braves even moved twice. They transferred from Boston, Massachusetts, to Milwaukee, Wisconsin, in 1953, then to Atlanta, Georgia, in 1966. Milwaukee was not without a team for long. The Seattle Pilots, which existed only in 1969, became the Milwaukee Brewers in 1970. But the most historically significant franchise shifts occurred in the late 1950s. In that era, several California cities had growing populations. The New York Giants moved to San Francisco. The Brooklyn Dodgers went to Los Angeles. That left New York with just one team, the Yankees, until the expansion Mets joined the NL in 1962. In 1972, the Washington, DC, Senators moved to Texas and became the Rangers. But baseball returned to the nation's capital when the Montreal Expos moved there in 2005 and became the Nationals.

CHAPTER

DEAD BALL, LIVE BALL, AND THE SULTAN OF SWAT

By the mid-1800s, baseball bore a resemblance to its modern version, but there were still significant differences. ▶

The beginnings of baseball remain shrouded in mystery. The theory that an American Civil War (1861–1865) hero named Abner Doubleday drew rules to the new game with a stick in the dust has been debunked. MLB official historian John Thorn believes variations of the sport were played in different areas of the United States as early as the 1700s.

Baseball in those days could hardly be recognized today. There was no such thing as a strike called by an umpire. Batters were out if a fielder caught the ball on one bounce or hit them with a thrown baseball as they raced to the next base. A hitter could demand a low or high pitch. The pitcher was forced to release the ball underhanded with both feet on the ground.

Amateur clubs began springing up throughout the country in the early 1800s. Some players were paid to play, but no team was composed entirely of professionals until the 1869 Cincinnati Red Stockings were formed. That club attracted the finest talent from coast to coast. They dominated the competition as a traveling team. They battered foes by scores such as 86–8, 53–0, 71–15, and 63–4. Few games were close as the Red Stockings finished the year with a 64–0 record.

The arrival of the Red Stockings often attracted huge crowds. An estimated 20,000 fans flocked to a ballpark in New York to watch them play the Brooklyn Atlantic club on June 14, 1870. The result was the first defeat for Cincinnati.

A promotional poster showed the 1869 lineup of the famous Cincinnati Red Stockings.

The *Cincinnati Daily Enquirer* wrote the following about the tension in the air as the battle went into extra innings:

> *The excitement was intense from beginning to last, the silence being so great at time[s] that one could hear the suppressed breathing of the players, and the vast crowd at time[s] . . . breaking out into the most tumultuous cheering ever heard on a ball ground. Nearly all our nine played splendidly, but they were beaten fairly and squarely.*[1]

BIRTH OF THE SENIOR CIRCUIT

Soon new professional franchises were born. That led to the failed National Association in 1871 and the formation of the NL in 1876. The basic structure of MLB had been developed. The most populous cities in the United States sported teams, including New York; Chicago, Illinois; Philadelphia, Pennsylvania; and Saint Louis, Missouri.

Early stars such as New York catcher Buck Ewing and Chicago first baseman Cap Anson attracted fans. But Anson and others launched a shameful period in baseball history that lasted six decades when they banned nonwhite players from the major leagues. African Americans were forced to form their own teams and travel around the country seeking competition.

The composition of professional baseball continued to change. The American Association served as the main rival to the NL from 1882 until it folded in 1891. The current MLB

The crowd came onto the field after the first game of the 1903 World Series, a best-of-nine series in which the Boston Pilgrims beat the Pittsburgh Pirates.

structure was born with the formation of the major league AL in 1901 and the advent of the World Series two years later, in 1903.

But the game remained quite different from the version played in the modern era. Perhaps the most striking difference was a lack of home runs. Most home runs before the 1900s did not fly over fences. They scooted between outfielders and allowed batters to sprint around the bases. The number of home runs dropped even more markedly in the early 1900s. The balls would get covered up with dirt during the game, and umpires didn't replace the balls as frequently as they do today. This made them harder to see and hit as daylight faded. The baseballs also got softened up as they took a beating all game long. These factors resulted in fewer home runs. Even the most powerful sluggers rarely hit more than ten home runs in a season. One Philadelphia star, John Franklin Baker, earned the nickname "Home Run Baker."[2] He led the AL in home runs in four straight seasons, never hitting more than 12 per season during that stretch. The period became known as the Dead-ball era.

The lack of home runs did not prevent the emergence of incredible offensive talent. Feisty Detroit star Ty Cobb and his Pittsburgh counterpart Honus Wagner remain among the greatest hitters of all time. They battled against legendary pitchers such as Washington flamethrower Walter "Big Train" Johnson, New York Giants star Christy Mathewson, and crafty Cy Young, whose major league record of 511 pitching victories is almost certain to remain unbroken.

BRING ON THE BABE

In the 1920s, one man changed baseball forever. He had arrived on the scene with the Boston Red Sox as a dominant pitcher. George Herman "Babe" Ruth helped that team win a few World Series in the 1910s on the mound. But his power

MLB IN 1903

AMERICAN LEAGUE

Boston
Americans

Chicago
White Sox

Cleveland
Naps

Detroit
Tigers

New York
Highlanders

Philadelphia
Athletics

Saint Louis
Browns

Washington
Senators

NATIONAL LEAGUE

Boston
Beaneaters

Brooklyn
Superbas

Chicago
Cubs

Cincinnati
Reds

New York
Giants

Philadelphia
Phillies

Pittsburgh
Pirates

Saint Louis
Cardinals

TY
COBB

The greatest hitter in baseball history? It is arguably Detroit Tigers outfielder Ty Cobb. The nastiest player in baseball history? It could be the same guy. Cobb led the AL in batting average 12 times, including nine straight seasons from 1907 to 1915. He still owns the record for highest career batting average at .366. Cobb played with a burning desire to win. But he was plagued with a terrible temper on and off the field. He would slam into infielders with his spiked cleats. He once attacked a disabled heckler in the stands. He was even charged with attempted murder after a fight with a hotel watchman. Cobb was elected into the National Baseball Hall of Fame. But he remains one of the most infamous figures in the history of the sport.

◄ Cobb warms up on the field before a 1922 game.

as a hitter was already clear. He shattered the single-season home run record with 29 in 1919. No other player hit more than 12 that year. Ruth was developing into the greatest superstar in the sport. But Red Sox owner Harry Frazee needed money, so he sold Ruth to the New York Yankees before the 1920 season.

The controversial deal shifted the balance of power in baseball as Ruth ushered in a new era. Fans poured into ballparks to watch the player nicknamed The Sultan of Swat smash pitches over the fence. Owners began to understand the lure of the home run. The Dead-ball era was soon over, and the so-called Live-ball era began. Other players began to compile huge home run totals as well. Nobody hit as many as Ruth, who teamed with iconic first baseman Lou Gehrig to help the Yankees create the first dynasty in baseball history. New York won six AL pennants and three

THEY WERE ALL-STARS

Chicago mayor Edward J. Kelly wanted to arrange a sporting event for the 1933 World's Fair, an exhibition being planned for his city. *Chicago Tribune* sports editor Arch Ward hatched a plan. He organized the first All-Star Game, a battle between the best players from the AL and NL. A crowd of 47,595 packed Comiskey Park to watch a game that featured such greats as Babe Ruth and Jimmie Foxx.[3] Ruth sparked a 4–2 American League victory with a home run. The All-Star Game has been an annual highlight of the baseball season ever since.

World Series titles from 1921 to 1928. The 1927 club is still considered perhaps the greatest ever assembled.

The team known as the Bronx Bombers had no monopoly on superstars. The growing popularity of the sport in the 1920s was also driven by Hall of Famers such as Saint Louis slugger Rogers Hornsby, Chicago Cubs center fielder Hack Wilson, New York Giants right fielder Mel Ott, and Jimmie Foxx, who starred for both the Philadelphia Athletics and Boston Red Sox. Several pitchers also shone, including Athletics star Lefty Grove and right-hander Dizzy Dean, who led the Saint Louis Cardinals to two World Series crowns in the early 1930s. But the era was dominated by home run sluggers who sent fans flocking to the ballparks.

THE GREAT GASHOUSE GANG

They had colorful personalities and colorful nicknames. They wore unwashed uniforms. They were loud and annoying. They fought with each other and against opposing teams. They were led by hitters Joe "Ducky" Medwick, James "Ripper" Collins, and Johnny "Pepper" Martin, as well as pitching brothers Jay Hanna "Dizzy" Dean and Paul "Daffy" Dean. They were the 1934 Saint Louis Cardinals. But they were also known as the Gashouse Gang. The nickname grew from a boast by Cardinals players that they could beat any AL team in a World Series. Shortstop Leo "The Lip" Durocher added, "They wouldn't even let us in that league over there. They think we're a bunch of gas housers."[4] The name referred to foul-smelling factories that turned coal into gas. The Gashouse Gang backed up their boasts by beating Detroit in the World Series.

The attraction of baseball in that era began to take a back seat to other issues as the 1930s began. Most fans could not afford to spend their money on entertainment. The economic times were changing for the worse in America during this period. And baseball suffered for it.

CHAPTER 3

FROM THE FORTIES TO FREE AGENCY

Jackie Robinson, *left*, was the first black player in the modern MLB era. Integration was one of many changes the league underwent in the years after World War II. ▶

More than ten million fans attended major league baseball games in 1930. It marked the first time that milestone had been reached. The rising popularity of the sport promised even more clicks through the turnstiles in years to come.

But events outside the world of sports sent attendance reeling. The Great Depression, a prolonged economic downturn that began in 1929, gripped America. Millions struggled to find the money to put food on their tables or keep a roof over their heads. They certainly could not afford tickets to a ball game. Attendance soon tumbled. Only six million showed up to major league parks in 1933. That translated to fewer than 5,000 per game.[1] The Depression continued to bring misery through most of the decade. Fans listened to games on the radio rather than attending in person.

The launching of World War II (1939–1945) again diverted attention from baseball. A war that began in Europe and Asia reached the United States when the Japanese bombed Pearl Harbor, a US naval base in Hawaii, on December 7, 1941. The United States declared war on that country and was soon embroiled in the conflict in Europe as well. Superstars such as Cleveland pitcher Bob Feller, Yankees slugger Joe DiMaggio, and emerging Boston standout Ted Williams left the sport to join the military. Teams tried to piece together rosters without much of their top talent.

From left, MLB players Joseph Coleman, John F. Sain, Ted Williams, Johnny Pesky, and Louis Gremp underwent flight training as part of their military service during World War II.

MLB marched ahead. But the quality of the game suffered, and millions of fans had either become soldiers or lost interest in the sport.

The most destructive war in history, which ended in 1945, left the victorious United States as the most prosperous nation on Earth. Players and fans returned home and streamed back to the ballparks in record numbers. Attendance nearly doubled. But not all who fought for America in World War II were provided equal opportunities. African American players remained on the outside looking in. Many of the premier baseball talents in the United States

THE ONE-ARMED OUTFIELDER

Among the most amazing success stories in MLB history was that of Pete Gray, who played outfield for the Saint Louis Browns in 1945. Gray lost his right arm at age 12, when it was run over by a pickup truck. He played in 77 games and sported a .218 batting average swinging with only his left arm. He would catch the baseball with a glove that he then placed on the stump under his right shoulder so he could throw the ball back.

were forced to compete in separate organizations known as the Negro Leagues. There were no official rules against black players joining major league clubs. But an unwritten agreement among owners prevented integration until 1946. That is when Brooklyn Dodgers owner Branch Rickey decided to break through the racial barrier and sign a courageous and brilliant athlete named Jackie Robinson.

Robinson had starred in football, baseball, and track at the University of California, Los Angeles before joining the Negro American League's Kansas City Monarchs. He played in the minor leagues in 1946, breaking the color barrier there. After signing with the Dodgers, he was ready to play in MLB in the 1947 season. A group of Brooklyn teammates threatened to refuse to play with him. Opposing players said they would boycott games against the Dodgers unless Robinson was benched. Players from the segregated South were especially brutal. Robinson was taunted mercilessly.

Opposing players spit on him. But one reason Rickey had signed him was because of his emotional toughness. Robinson did not just survive; he thrived, winning NL Rookie of the Year honors and forging a Hall of Fame career.

MASS INTEGRATION

Soon other black players were joining major league clubs. One was Cleveland outfielder Larry Doby, who became the first black American Leaguer and also earned a spot in the Hall of Fame. Another was Giants star outfielder Monte Irvin, who appreciated what Robinson achieved for other African American players.

"Jackie Robinson opened the door of baseball to all men," Irvin said after Robinson died in 1972. "He was the first to get the opportunity, but if he had not done such a great job, the path would have been so much more difficult. . . . Jack was the trailblazer and we are all deeply grateful."[2]

The influx of African American players markedly increased the level of talent in the major leagues. Now that the best players all got a chance to play, regardless of their race, new superstars emerged. Those included the Giants' Willie Mays, whom many still consider the greatest player of all time. Milwaukee Braves outfielder Hank Aaron, whose team moved to Atlanta in 1966, began a successful attack on the all-time career home run record of 714 set by Ruth.

Monte Irvin followed Robinson into MLB, joining the New York Giants in 1949.

None of that changed a reality that proved disturbing to fans outside New York—the Yankees continued to dominate the sport. They won 15 of 18 American League pennants and ten World Series championships from 1947 to 1964. The Yankees continued to sign premier talent before the advent of the amateur draft in 1965 evened out the playing field. In 1951 they added Mickey Mantle, who boasted incredible power and speed, and they supplemented his greatness with strong players throughout a powerful lineup. And, led by right-handed ace Whitey Ford, they had enough pitching to hold off strong charges from contenders nearly every year.

THE DOMINANT HURLERS

Ford was far from the only pitcher dominating the sport in the late 1950s and 1960s. A new generation of brilliant hurlers such as Juan Marichal of the Giants, Bob Gibson of the Cardinals, and the Dodgers' Sandy Koufax and Don Drysdale helped lower scores of games considerably. Teams of the 1960s began averaging four runs per game or fewer for the first time since before Ruth launched an offensive

THE CATCH

The Cleveland Indians set an AL record with 111 wins in 1954. They had halted the Yankees dynasty for one season. And they were heavily favored to defeat the New York Giants in the World Series. In the eighth inning of Game 1 at the Polo Grounds in New York, the score was tied 2–2 when Cleveland's first two runners reached base. Up stepped Indians slugger Vic Wertz, who bashed a booming drive to deep center field. It seemed impossible that even the speedy Willie Mays could reach the ball. But the Giants center fielder sprinted with his back to home plate and made an over-the-shoulder catch some 420 feet (128 m) from home plate.[3] He then turned around while falling back and fired the ball to the infield to keep the runners from scoring. Many consider it the greatest grab in baseball history. It has forever been known simply as "The Catch." The Giants won the game in extra innings and went on to sweep the Indians in four games.

era nearly a half century earlier. Many fans considered such low-scoring games boring. Attendance dropped considerably. MLB had to do something to attract fans who yearned to see more action. So it lowered the mound five inches (13 cm) in 1969 to make it tougher on pitchers. The move worked. Soon more players were hitting the ball and more fans were coming to watch.

Those players were also a little richer. They won a major battle against the team owners in the 1970s. Major league players for generations had been tied to a common line in their contracts known as the reserve clause. It forced them to remain with the same team until they were traded or released. The lack of freedom was matched by a lack of pay. The minimum annual salary was a mere $6,000 in 1967. The average salary was just $19,000.[4] The MLB Players Association decided to act by hiring economist and contract negotiator Marvin

SUPER SANDY

Dodgers left-hander Sandy Koufax struggled in the early part of his career. He owned a blistering fastball and sharp-breaking curve but could control neither. He averaged more than a strikeout per inning in the late 1950s, which was a rare feat in that era. But he walked too many batters. His career was foundering. Then he found his control and became perhaps the greatest pitcher of all time. Koufax sported a 111–34 record over his last five seasons and led the NL in earned run average in all of them. Arm troubles forced him to retire at age 30.

Miller to represent it in talks with the owners. The persistent Miller kept battling at the negotiation table and in the courts. He finally gained free agency for the players in 1975. This meant they could sell their services to the highest bidder. The average salary of major league players skyrocketed to $143,000 by 1980.[5]

But even that was pocket change compared with what they would soon be earning. Free agency changed the face of baseball. The battles between the players and owners had just begun. This would lead to resentment from some fans, who believed both sides to be greedy. But despite the growing tension on the labor front, the players were still providing great baseball. The game had never been more popular.

CHAPTER

CREATING THE MODERN GAME

The Seattle Mariners, playing at the Kingdome stadium, were one of the MLB teams added to the league in ▶ the 1970s.

S ome baseball fans feared in the 1970s that their favorite sport was headed for disaster. They believed free agency would allow wealthier teams to buy their way to success. Meanwhile, clubs with less money would suffer.

Those worries proved only somewhat justified. MLB enjoyed greater parity after the advent of free agency. No franchise has forged an extended dynasty since that of the Yankees ended in 1964. But the ability to sign the finest talent has helped richer clubs stay strong. Teams such as the Yankees and Dodgers need not rely solely on developing their own players in their minor league systems to remain pennant contenders. They can spend hundreds of millions of dollars on premier free agents. Meanwhile, top players leave teams that can no longer afford them.

But though the majority of World Series crowns are won by teams with larger payrolls, many small-market teams have thrived by drafting the best amateur players, developing strong minor league systems, and making shrewd trades. Cleveland won three AL pennants from 1995 to 2016. Kansas City captured World Series crowns in 1985 and 2015. The Oakland Athletics earned three consecutive trips to the Fall Classic and won it all in 1989.

THE GROWING MAJOR LEAGUES

Expansion has changed the landscape for all major league teams. The AL and NL consisted of just eight clubs each

Kansas City Royals players celebrate after winning the 1985 World Series, a victory that helped prove teams with lower budgets could survive and thrive in MLB.

through 1960 and then ten through 1968. There were no playoffs. The top team in each league played in the World Series to determine the champion. The addition of new franchises resulted in leagues split into divisions and the first-ever playoff rounds. There have been 30 MLB teams since 1998. Teams must win at least three rounds of playoff games to snag a World Series crown. With the advent of the playoff system, eight more clubs received the opportunity to play for a title than did before 1969.

The larger playoff field did not prevent several of the greatest teams in baseball history from proving their dominance. Among them were the Cincinnati Reds of the 1970s. So powerful was their offense that they became known as the Big Red Machine. Their lineup featured all-time greats such as catcher Johnny Bench, first baseman Tony Perez, second baseman Joe Morgan, and outfielders Pete Rose and George Foster. The Reds won World Series crowns in 1975 and 1976.

Cincinnati's mini-dynasty was followed by another one. The Yankees of the late 1970s, managed by feisty Billy Martin, squabbled among themselves. Superstar slugger Reggie Jackson engaged in heated verbal spats with Martin

THE GREATEST GAME OF ALL TIME?

Game 6 of the 1975 World Series between Boston and Cincinnati has been called the greatest ever. The Reds needed one more win at Boston's iconic Fenway Park to take the crown. Red Sox pinch hitter Bernie Carbo tied it at 6–6 with a three-run homer in the eighth inning. The score remained knotted into the twelfth inning. That's when Boston catcher Carlton Fisk mashed a pitch down the left field line. He waved his arms to the right to will the ball fair. It indeed stayed fair for the game-winning home run. But Cincinnati won Game 7 to take the series.

in the dugout during games for all to see. Controversial Yankees owner George Steinbrenner argued with Martin through the media and even fired him five times from 1975 to 1988. But Martin guided the team to playoff success in the late 1970s. And Jackson played the role of hero when championships were on the line. He slammed five home runs in a 1977 World Series defeat of the Dodgers, including three in one game. He sported an incredible batting average of .429 in the 1977 Fall Classic and 1978 playoffs combined. It is no wonder Jackson was nicknamed Mr. October. He was perhaps the greatest clutch player ever.

The short-lived dynasties of the Reds and Yankees were followed by the most pronounced period of parity in baseball history. Seventeen different teams played in the World Series from 1980 to 1992, and only the Dodgers and Minnesota Twins won more than one World Series during that stretch. The result was that fans in more cities could excitedly follow their teams as they played for championships.

The 1980s and early 1990s featured great pure hitters rather than power hitters. Boston third baseman Wade Boggs and San Diego outfielder Tony Gwynn slashed line drives all over the field. Oakland Athletics and Yankees standout Rickey Henderson could hit the ball a long way but mostly drove pitchers crazy by reaching base with singles and walks before stealing second and third. Henderson led

Rickey Henderson slides for his 939th stolen base in 1991, breaking the MLB record.

the AL in stolen bases 12 times and finished with a major league record 1,406 steals during his Hall of Fame career. Such hitters and base stealers brought excitement to the game.

But baseball was having many problems. Among them was that football had surpassed it in overall popularity among American sports fans. They perceived the pace of baseball as too slow. Another issue was the labor strife that continued to haunt the sport and cause significant stoppages in 1981 and 1994, the second of which w out the end of the regular season, the playoffs, and the World Series.

THE HOME RUN CHASE

Baseball needed a jolt of energy, and it received one in the late 1990s. It came with the chase of arguably the most hallowed record in sports—the single-season home run mark of 61, established in 1961 by Yankees slugger Roger Maris. Teams began consistently averaging more than one home run per game for the first time in baseball history. Players who had displayed little power began blasting baseballs 400 feet (122 m). Among them was Baltimore outfielder Brady Anderson, who had never hit more than 21 home runs in a single season before smashing 50 in 1996. Fans and the media accused MLB of using harder balls that traveled

THE NEW IRON MAN

Baltimore third baseman Cal Ripken Jr. was not the best talent of his generation. But he was a great player who achieved immortality. He broke the record of legendary Yankees first baseman Lou Gehrig by playing in 2,632 consecutive games. Gehrig, who died tragically young, had earned the nickname of "Iron Man" by playing in 2,130 straight. Ripken shattered the mark on September 6, 1995, and he continued adding to his total for three more years. Balloons in the Orioles' colors of orange and black were released into the air at his home ballpark of Camden Yards when he broke the record. Ripken then jogged around the stadium, shaking hands with fans.

Mark McGwire blasted his 53rd home run of the 1998 season in a late August game against the Pirates.

farther. Rumors began leaking out that players were taking illegal performance enhancing drugs to gain power.

But none of that seemed to matter in 1998. That is when Chicago Cubs outfielder Sammy Sosa and Saint Louis Cardinals first baseman Mark McGwire provided drama by staging an all-out assault on the Maris home run record. Both began blasting baseballs at an incredible rate. Fans who had been turned off by the strike that killed the 1994 season streamed back to ballparks.

Both Sosa and McGwire had shattered the Maris mark by mid-September. The drama continued as the nation focused on which player would hold the new mark. McGwire earned that distinction when he smashed five home runs over the last weekend of the season to finish with 70 to Sosa's 66.

Meanwhile, San Francisco superstar outfielder Barry Bonds followed the chase with interest and a bit of anger. He too yearned for the national attention McGwire and Sosa had received. Bonds bulked up further—most believe all three players used steroids to help achieve their power numbers—and clobbered 73 home runs in 2001. Bonds continued to smash home runs. In 2007 he overcame the career mark of 755 set by Hank Aaron in 1974.

Many believed the game had changed for the worse. Some fans became bored with players swinging for the fences and the huge increase in home runs that peaked at

BETTERING BABE

Few believed in the 1950s that Hank Aaron could overtake Babe Ruth as the most prolific home run hitter of all time. Many figured Willie Mays and Mickey Mantle were more viable candidates. But their home run paces slowed down in the 1960s. Aaron continued to smash them into the 1970s to place himself at 713 career home runs after the 1973 season. He faced incredible pressure as 1974 approached. The national spotlight was nothing compared with the hate mail. He received death threats from racists who despised the notion of a black man owning perhaps the most sacred record in sports. But Aaron wasn't fazed. He wasted no time in tying the record of 714 with a homer on opening day in Cincinnati. Four days later he hit number 715 in front of his home fans in Atlanta off Dodgers left-hander Al Dowling.

MIKE
TROUT

Mike Trout did not receive extensive media attention during his first nine years in the major leagues. He was not one to seek the spotlight. And the Angels team on which he played reached the playoffs only once during that period. But Trout was compared early in his career to Hall of Famer Mickey Mantle, who starred with the Yankees in the 1950s and 1960s. The comparison was made because Trout exhibited an incredible combination of speed and power. And he did nothing over the next several years to weaken that comparison. Trout finished first or second in the AL MVP voting an incredible seven times in eight seasons and won Rookie of the Year honors in 2012, when he led the league in runs scored and bases stolen. Trout led the league four times in runs scored and in on-base percentage, which measures how often a hitter reaches base by hit or walk.

Though his team has not found postseason success, Trout has posted dominant statistics in his time with the Angels.

46

2.78 per game in 2019. They became bored with strikeouts that reached a rate of about one per half-inning. There were more strikeouts than hits for the first time in baseball history in 2018. Then it happened again in 2019. Games once lasted an average of two hours. Now, they were often taking more than three hours to complete. There was too much time between pitches. Fans craved more action.

It seemed that baseball featured as many great athletes as ever. Hitters such as Los Angeles Angels outfielder Mike Trout, Cleveland shortstop Francisco Lindor, Los Angeles Dodgers first baseman Cody Bellinger, and Milwaukee outfielder Christian Yelich had an amazing mix of speed and power. Premier pitchers such as Washington ace Max Scherzer and Houston star Justin Verlander continued to baffle opposing hitters. Pitchers were throwing harder than ever. Several could fire baseballs at more than 100 miles per hour (161 kmh).

But MLB had an identity problem. It was failing to successfully market its superstars. It had been said that the great Trout, a three-time AL most valuable player (MVP), could walk down the street of most American cities and not be recognized. Only time would tell whether a sport with passionate fans since the 1860s could ever regain its status as the national pastime.

CHAPTER 5

DOWN ON THE FARM

Minor league teams, such as the Rochester Red Wings, are filled with players hoping to earn their way into MLB. ▸

Today's major league players earn an average of nearly $5 million a year.[1] They compete before an average of nearly 30,000 fans in ballparks and millions more on television.[2] Many receive endorsement deals. The best are showered with fame and fortune. They are the toast of major cities throughout America and even in Toronto, Canada, the one city outside the United States with an MLB team.

These players are the fortunate few. Most professional ballplayers toil in comparative anonymity. They are the minor leaguers hoping for a shot at the big leagues, sometimes known as The Show. Every major league franchise grooms its hopeful talent in minor league systems. Most of those players never come close to reaching the parent club. They barely make enough money for food and rent. And they are unable to prove themselves talented enough to play in the big leagues. Their dreams are dashed, and they quit baseball.

That is the sad reality. Only about one in ten professional players ever plays a major league game.[3] Those with the most drive and determination to work tirelessly on their skills maximize their chances to reach the majors. They must have enough talent to succeed at the highest level. But many must also be lucky. Those in organizations headed by bad major league teams are often provided with greater opportunities to be promoted. Clubs that are weaker in

Players with the minor league Saint Paul Saints take part in batting practice in 1942.

certain positions are more likely to bring up minor leaguers who play those spots on the field.

Minor leagues began to spring up in the 1880s. But the National Association of Professional Baseball Leagues, which is also simply known as the minors, was not affiliated with the major leagues. It was launched with 14 leagues and 96 teams in 1902 and continued to grow. It expanded to 41 leagues by 1914 before falling victim to raids by the new Federal League and the loss of manpower during World War I (1914–1918). Only nine leagues remained in

1918. An agreement was reached three years later that allowed MLB clubs to own minor league teams and establish farm systems.

The result was vast expansion. Major league franchises added dozens of farm teams in the 1930s and 1940s. They often owned several clubs at the same level. From 1946 to 1962, when the current minor league system was created, there were six classes of minor leagues. Class AAA was the highest, followed by AA, A, B, C, and D. At its peak in 1949, minor league baseball featured 59 leagues and nearly 450 teams. Almost 40 million fans attended minor league games that year.[4]

A NEW SYSTEM

The advent of television gave fans another entertainment outlet and had a devastating effect on minor league attendance in the 1950s. Fans could watch major league teams from the comfort of their living rooms. More people were listening to AL and NL games on the radio through national broadcasts. Minor leagues began to fold. Attendance dropped to 13.2 million in 1958, about one-third the number that had clicked through the turnstiles less than a decade earlier.[5]

The result was a restructuring that took effect in 1963 and has remained in place with few variations. Each major league club in the modern era owns one Triple-A team, one Double-A team, one Class A Advanced team, one Class A team, and at least two Rookie League teams. Some also run short-season teams in the lower minor leagues. Premier prospects rise in farm systems until they reach Triple-A, which is one step from the major leagues. Some of the very best prospects even skip Triple-A entirely.

Perhaps the most significant change to the system occurred in 1965 with the advent of the amateur draft. Major league franchises previously sent scouts throughout the country to find the top high school and college prospects. Scouts would report back, and teams would then decide whether they would offer contracts to recommended players. The June draft prevented teams from getting players they had scouted right away. They had to wait until that annual event to select them before they could sign them.

The expansion that has nearly doubled the number of major league franchises since 1960 has provided greater opportunity for eager baseball talent. The existence of more major league teams has resulted in more minor league teams. Minor league clubs have worked hard to attract fans by offering discounted tickets, additional entertainment between innings, and better food at concession stands. The result has been a boom in minor league attendance. More than 41 million fans attended minor league games in 2019.[6]

GOING THROUGH THE SYSTEM—OR NOT

Players selected in the amateur draft or young international talent that major league franchises sign are nearly always assigned to minor league teams. Rarely have players jumped from high school or college baseball into the majors. The draft round in which they were selected determines the amount of money offered as a signing bonus.

Draft status also affects the minor league level in which they are placed. Experienced college players chosen early in the first

THE FIRST FEMALE UMPIRES

Bernice Gera only umpired one minor league game. But that was enough to earn her fame as the first female umpire in professional baseball history. Gera worked a New York–Penn League game on June 24, 1972. Pam Postema lasted far longer. She worked her way through the minors and reached the Triple-A level as an umpire in 1987. But she was never offered a chance to umpire in the big leagues and was released in 1989.

round often skip Rookie League and even lower Class A to land in Class A Advanced or Double-A. But those fresh out of high school are most often assigned to Rookie League teams because they require the most additional experience before they are ready to advance.

The most effective minor league coaches and managers are the best teachers. Their jobs are to hone the skills of their players. The purpose of every minor league system is to prepare talent for the big leagues. Pitching coaches help starters and relievers throw strikes, tinker with their deliveries to increase fastball velocity, and create movement on pitches that makes hitters swing and miss. Minor league hitting coaches help their students make more consistent hard contact, learn enough patience to lay off balls out of the strike zone, and develop swings to add power. Fielding

RIGHT TO THE BIG LEAGUES

Only 21 players have made their professional debut in the majors since the 1965 draft, and none did it from 2010 to 2019. The practice was prevalent with pitchers in the early 1970s. Struggling teams such as the Cleveland Indians and Washington Senators (who moved to Texas in 1972) publicized the pitching debuts of high draft picks such as Steve Dunning, Pete Broberg, and David Clyde to attract fans. Big crowds attended those games, but the lack of minor league experience stunted the growth of those three pitchers and resulted in career failures. Several position players proved they needed no minor league seasoning. Among them was Hall of Fame outfielder Dave Winfield, who debuted with San Diego in 1973.

Minor league batting coach Hernan Iribarren works with his Billings Mustangs before a 2019 game.

coaches aid in taking the best routes to fly balls and ground balls, cutting down on errors, and making strong and accurate throws.

Talent is required to reach the major leagues. But players who are the most open to teaching and are able to incorporate it into their games generally advance faster through minor league systems. A huge majority of players spend their entire careers in the minors and eventually give up their pursuit. Fame and fortune is one motivator for those who keep striving for the top despite low pay and long bus rides from town to town. But the satisfaction and pride players feel once they step onto a major league field is also a huge motivation. Those that do make it know they have reached the highest level of the sport.

NEW YORK YANKEES
MINOR LEAGUE AFFILIATES

MAJOR LEAGUE
NEW YORK YANKEES

⬇

AAA
SCRANTON/WILKES-BARRE RAILRIDERS

⬇

AA
TRENTON THUNDER

⬇

ADVANCED A
TAMPA TARPONS

⬇

A
CHARLESTON RIVERDOGS

⬇

SHORT-SEASON A
STATEN ISLAND YANKEES

⬇

ROOKIE
GULF COAST LEAGUE YANKEES EAST
GULF COAST LEAGUE YANKEES WEST
PULASKI YANKEES

CHAPTER

RIVALRIES AND AWARDS

The rivalry between the Red Sox and Yankees is among the most celebrated in all of sports. ▶

The Chicago Bears and Green Bay Packers in pro football make up one of sports' biggest rivalries. The Boston Celtics and Los Angeles Lakers in pro basketball form another contender for that title. But many agree that the most intense rivalry has been played at Fenway Park and Yankee Stadium for a century. These are the battles between the Boston Red Sox and New York Yankees.

It all started when Boston owner Harry Frazee sold budding superstar Babe Ruth to the Yankees before the 1920 season. The Red Sox had won four World Series crowns in the previous eight years. They would not win another until 2004. The Yankees had never won a title until landing Ruth, who led them to four world championships and seven American League pennants over the next 13 seasons while the Red Sox became the worst team in baseball.

What became known as the Curse of the Bambino, a reference to one of Ruth's nicknames, haunted the Red Sox and their fans for more than 80 years. The Yankees embarked on a baseball dynasty that lasted four decades. And they battered Boston on the field with pennants on the line. The Red Sox, however, eventually enjoyed some revenge in later years.

The selling of Ruth had become a distant memory when Boston became a contender in the 1940s. One reason for the intensifying rivalry was the individual competition between Joe DiMaggio of the Yankees and Ted Williams of

Baseball legend Babe Ruth is at the center of the historic Red Sox–Yankees rivalry.

the Red Sox. Fans throughout the baseball world debated over which outfield superstar was superior.

The frustration felt by the Red Sox over head-to-head competition began in 1949. Boston won 11 straight games in September, including three in a row against the Yankees, to take over first place in the AL. The Sox needed just one win in New York to secure the AL pennant. Nearly 70,000 fans packed Yankee Stadium the next two days to watch the showdown.[1] The Red Sox blew a 4–0 lead in the first game and lost the second as well, allowing New York to sneak away with the title.

More misery was heaped upon the Sox and their fans in 1978. The team appeared set to run away with the AL East crown. They held a seven-game lead heading into September. But the Yankees chipped away at that lead before traveling to Fenway Park for a huge four-game series. The result became known as the Boston Massacre. New York outscored their rival 42–9 in sweeping the set and securing a tie for first place. The two teams finished the regular season in the same deadlock.

A one-game playoff was required to decide the AL champion. The Red Sox took a 2–0 lead into the seventh inning. Then light-hitting Yankees shortstop Bucky Dent shocked the baseball world by slugging a three-run homer to put his team ahead to stay. It was his first home run in seven weeks, but it gave his team the title. What many Sox fans perceived as the Curse of the Bambino had struck again.

Bucky Dent was not the last unheralded New York hitter to destroy the Sox with a playoff home run. Third baseman Aaron Boone slammed one in the eleventh inning of Game 7 of the 2003 AL Championship Series (ALCS) to send the Yankees to the Fall Classic and frustrate Boston fans yet again. Game 3 of that playoff battle was marred by a brawl in which Red Sox pitcher Pedro Martinez pushed

Physical fights have broken out at Red Sox–Yankees games multiple times in the rivalry's history, including in 2018.

72-year-old Yankees coach Don Zimmer to the ground. The ugly incident showed that the rivalry had reached its peak.

"I wish I'd never see them again," Martinez said of the Yankees. "I wish they'd disappear from the league. Then we'd be winners."[2]

The Curse of the Bambino, however, was soon to end. The Red Sox appeared destined to fall again to the Yankees in 2004 when they lost the first three games of the ALCS and trailed heading into the ninth inning of Game 4. But they rebounded to win that game and the next three to snag the pennant, and then they beat Saint Louis in the World Series. They had captured their first championship since 1918. And they had finally avenged their many defeats to New York along the way. The Red Sox became the most dominant team of the new century. They also won World Series titles in 2007, 2013, and 2018.

MLB features several other passionate rivalries. The San Francisco Giants and Los Angeles Dodgers have been rivals since both teams resided in New York. That rivalry had a highlight in the 1951 playoff battle but has remained strong based on history and their standing as the most consistent contenders in the NL West.

The Chicago Cubs and Saint Louis Cardinals also feature an intense competition based greatly on geography. Fans from both teams often make the trek to watch head-to-head competition in the opposing ballpark. But no rivalry can match that of the Yankees and Red Sox in history and intensity. It is a story with many chapters. And it did not die when Boston broke

THE QUAKE THAT STOPPED THE SERIES

Game 3 of the 1989 World Series between geographical rivals San Francisco and Oakland was about to begin. But suddenly the earth began to shake at Candlestick Park, home of the Giants. The Loma Prieta Earthquake had struck. It lasted just 17 seconds but caused 63 deaths and tremendous damage in the Bay Area.[3] The World Series was halted. Players on both sides helped the people of the two cities with the recovery effort. The series resumed ten days later, and Oakland would go on to complete a four-game sweep.

the Curse of the Bambino. Baseball fans cannot imagine that it will ever end.

ALL ABOUT AWARDS

Rivalries are not restricted to team competition. Baseball is all about the battle between pitcher and batter. But that one-on-one struggle does not just contribute to winning and losing games. The individual nature of the sport also plays a role in deciding who wins the many awards that are handed out after every season. Fans and even players often engage in heated debate over who deserves to be honored.

The most prestigious of all is the MVP Award, which is earned in both the AL and NL. The MVP Award is usually given to a hitter with the best combination of batting average, home runs, and runs batted in (RBI). A few hitters in baseball history have led their leagues in all three categories to win what is known as the Triple Crown. But even that does not ensure an MVP Award. Red Sox superstar Ted Williams earned the Triple Crown in 1942 and 1947 but failed to win MVP in either season. The voting is done by media members who also consider fielding prowess and the success of the candidates' teams.

Pitchers who have completed incredible seasons have won MVP Awards. But they also have a separate honor of their own. That is the Cy Young Award, which also is handed out by both leagues. It was named after the Hall of Fame

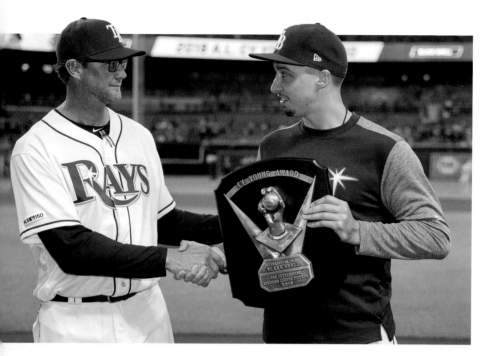

Tampa Bay Rays pitcher Blake Snell, *right*, won the 2018 Cy Young Award.

pitcher of the early 1900s. Pitchers with different styles have dominated Cy Young voting in their eras. Flame-throwing Roger Clemens earned seven from 1986 to 2004. Randy Johnson, who fired 100-mile-an-hour (161 kmh) fastballs, won five Cy Young Awards from 1995 to 2002, including a stretch of four in a row. But softer-throwing Greg Maddux, who kept hitters off balance with pinpoint control and changes of speed, won four straight from 1992 to 1995.

Another coveted award is Manager of the Year, which was established in 1983. That vote most often goes to the manager in each league who guided a team to the playoffs or transformed a bad club into a good one. Earning that honor does not ensure long-term employment. Most managers are fired soon after their teams stop reaching the expectations of the team ownership. The average tenure of a major league manager is less than four seasons.

MLB hands out many other postseason awards. The top fielders at each position win Gold Gloves. The premier relief pitcher—generally the closer who saves the most victories—is also honored. The player who best rebounds from injury or a poor season to have a good one earns Comeback Player of the Year.

The criteria many voters use to select baseball awards have changed. The advent of analytics has altered how players are judged. Analytics are advanced statistics. They give a deeper insight into players than simple numbers such as pitching wins or batting average. The science of analytics has permeated all levels of MLB. Teams hire analytics experts to help their scouts judge the skills, potential, and tendencies of their own players, opposing players, and prospects.

GOING PLATINUM

The best fielders at each position every season win Gold Glove Awards. But the one player deemed to be the premier fielder in each league does even better than that. He earns what is known as the Platinum Glove, an honor first bestowed in 2011. Stalwart Saint Louis catcher Yadier Molina owned an impressive four Platinum Gloves in 2019. Colorado Rockies third baseman Nolan Arenado won three straight from 2017 to 2019.

CHAPTER

THE SEASON STRUCTURE

Today's MLB season includes 162 games, the most of any professional sports league.

The World Series was once notable for the fact that the opposing teams could meet only in this championship series. AL teams and NL teams did not play each other during the regular season. That helped make baseball unique among major American sports.

But the desire to increase attendance in the regular season spurred MLB to action in 1997. That is when it launched interleague play. The initial plan created rivalries based on geography. For instance, teams in the AL East played only opponents in the NL East. Some interleague battles that featured teams from the same city, such as the New York Mets versus the New York Yankees or the Chicago White Sox versus the Chicago Cubs, drew large crowds. So did games pitting teams in the same area of the country against each other, such as the Kansas City Royals versus the Saint Louis Cardinals.

The format changed in 2002. That is when all major league teams began alternating divisions in interleague play while maintaining geographical rivalries. That allowed them to face every opponent from the other league every three years.

Some baseball fans have complained about interleague games. They believe after more than 20 years that these matchups have lost the freshness that once made them highly anticipated events. Such fans also claim that they have taken away what has historically made the World Series

THEY NEVER HAD A CHANCE

Several cities aside from New York and Chicago featured two major league teams into the 1950s. The NL's Boston Braves competed with the Red Sox until moving to Milwaukee in 1953. The AL's Philadelphia Athletics shared that city with the Phillies before relocating to Kansas City in 1955. And the AL's Saint Louis Browns competed with the Cardinals until moving to Baltimore in 1954. Only once did those teams compete against their same-city rival. That was when the Cardinals defeated the Browns in the 1944 World Series.

special. Critics of interleague competition cite that some Fall Classic foes have already played each other in the regular season. They point out that scheduling interleague games means fewer games are played between league rivals.

Such debates have led to other concerns about the unbalanced schedule, which was adopted by MLB in 2013. That schedule results in each team playing division opponents 19 times. It leaves just one home and one road series against every other team in the league. Fans have protested that they get tired of watching the same opponents. Some also believe the unbalanced schedule is unfair. It punishes teams that play in stronger divisions by forcing them to compete against those opponents far more often. But others feel that head-to-head battles against division foes, especially late in the season, add excitement to the pennant races.

A 2001 interleague game featured the Toronto Blue Jays and the Atlanta Braves.

EVOLUTION OF THE MLB SCHEDULE

MLB embraces tradition. The result for decades was little change in scheduling. A 154-game schedule was launched in 1904—three years after the birth of the AL—and remained in place for more than five decades. Each league consisted of eight teams that played each other 22 times every year.

The early popularity of baseball resulted in an increasing game count. The NL doubled its schedule from 70 games in 1876 to 140 by 1901. It even featured 154-game schedules in three seasons during that period. Expansion in the early 1960s motivated MLB to establish a 162-game slate. That number has remained in place ever since.

But much changed during that time, well before interleague play. The addition of two teams to each league in 1969 resulted in a two-division alignment. No longer did every team play each opponent the same number of times. They faced their division foes 18 times and non-division opponents 12 times every season. Many variations have been in place since, but MLB has always tried to prioritize divisional rivalries in its scheduling formula.

Many fans believe the regular season is simply too long. They suggest that it should go back to 154 games or even fewer. They cite early-season issues such as freezing weather

A SCHEDULING SOLUTION?

A solution has been often suggested to prevent early-season games from being postponed due to snow or cold weather: scheduling all early-season games in warm-weather cities or having teams with indoor or domed stadiums host them. But MLB continues to resist taking what many consider to be a logical step. The result has been many games postponed due to cold weather that must be played later in the season. That often causes problems as teams must find ways to squeeze games into tight schedules.

that affect the quality of play and the fan experience. The 162-game schedule forces teams to play in late March and early April, when cold temperatures remain and snow often continues to fall in some parts of the country.

HISTORY OF THE PLAYOFFS

The regular season once left two teams standing—the AL and NL winners. There were no playoffs through 1968. The World Series determined the champion. But expansion and the desire for MLB and its clubs to make more money from ticket sales and national television revenue changed the landscape of the postseason. A playoff system was launched in 1969 and has been consistently expanding ever since.

It began with one round. The two division winners in both leagues competed in a best of five playoff beginning in 1969. The series became best of seven in 1985. The winners of those series met in the World Series. The expansion to three divisions in the AL and NL in 1994 again altered the format. Not only did all three division winners earn playoff berths but so did the second-place club with the best record. This wild card team played the division champion with the best record in a best of five series. The other two division winners also played a best of five series. The survivors of those played a best of seven league championship series to qualify for the Fall Classic.

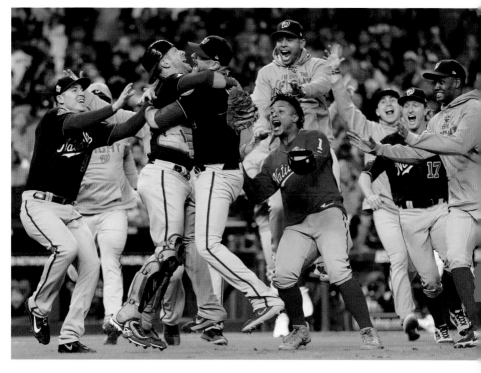

The wild card system made it possible for a team like the 2019 Washington Nationals to reach and win the World Series.

Eight playoff teams were not enough for MLB. The league yearned to add more postseason revenue. Those who ran the sport also understood that additional qualifiers created excitement in more cities during the regular season. A second wild card team was added in both leagues in 2012. The two wild card clubs faced off in a one-game battle for the right to continue in the playoffs. They needed to win four rounds to snag a World Series title. But it was proven possible. The 2014 San Francisco Giants and 2019 Washington Nationals have both won World Series crowns as wild card qualifiers since the new format was introduced.

There was no doubt that expanded playoffs brought greater excitement to more fans in more cities. This was especially true in comparison with the years before 1969, when many pennant races were over by early September. But some baseball purists have complained about the steady increase in playoff teams. They believe it cheapens the regular season.

What is certain is that dynasties such as that of the Yankees from the 1920s into the 1960s are unlikely to be repeated. The requirement to win at least three series to earn a championship makes such extended dominance less likely. No team has even won two straight World Series titles since the turn of the century.

GOOD BASEBALL TOWNS, BAD BASEBALL TOWNS

Perhaps the truest test of how well a city supports its franchise can be found in season attendance when its team wins. Some cities have passed that test. The New York Yankees, Los Angeles Dodgers, and Saint Louis Cardinals have consistently won on the field and ranked among the top teams in attendance.

Other teams have failed to draw well despite strength on the field. Among them have been the Tampa Bay Rays. They earned five playoff berths from 2008 to 2019 but have finished in the bottom four in the AL in attendance in all but

THE BEST BASEBALL TOWN IN NORTH AMERICA?

Which city boasts the best baseball fans in the United States? It is a subjective question. But in 2017 Fox Sports set out to find an answer by examining different criteria and publishing a list ranking the best. The organization studied attendance figures, jersey sales, and competition from other major sports. The report concluded that Saint Louis was the best baseball town in North America.[2] It was not the first time that claim had been made. The Saint Louis Cardinals have won 23 pennants and 11 World Series, totals higher than those of any other NL team. They drew more than three million fans every year but one from 1998 to 2019. They have not finished in the bottom half of the NL in attendance since 1980. Winning certainly helps. The Cardinals have finished with a losing record just once since the turn of the century.

one of those seasons. The Rays placed last in AL attendance six times in seven years from 2013 to 2019 despite reaching the postseason twice. The Miami Marlins also ranked at or near the bottom in NL attendance even with winning teams. In one 2019 game, the team drew just over 5,000 fans, a few hundred more than one of the team's minor league affiliates drew on the same night.[1] The struggles of the Rays and Marlins to attract fans have led some to conclude that MLB cannot succeed in Florida.

CHAPTER

STRIKES, SCANDALS, AND STEROIDS

From the 1960s to the 1980s, Marvin Miller helped
represent MLB players in disputes with team owners. ▶

MLB would have preferred over the years that the action on the field had captured all the attention. But this has not been the case. Battles between players and owners have instead grabbed many of the headlines. Players have sought more money and the freedom to sell their services to the highest bidder. Owners have fought them every step of the way. The result has been bitterness between the two sides when negotiating new collective bargaining agreements. And it has on several occasions resulted in strikes or lockouts that have taken baseball away from millions of fans.

Such problems are nearly as old as organized baseball itself. Players even complained about a lack of freedom in the late 1800s. The result was leagues that competed against the NL, such as the American Association, which ran from 1882 to 1891. Other options included leagues formed and run by players, such as the Players League. But only the NL stayed alive. At this time, an element of contracts called the reserve clause tied players to one team unless they were released or traded. It prevented player freedom into the 1970s.

The MLB Players Association (MLBPA) was born in 1953. But it was not officially recognized as a union until 1966. That is when it hired economist and contract negotiator Marvin Miller to represent its members. Miller went to work to allow players to negotiate with teams for more money. He fought for free agency. He battled the owners at the bargaining table and in courts. The owners battled back. But in December 1975 the reserve clause was on its way out. An independent arbitrator ruled in favor of free agency for pitchers Andy Messersmith and Dave McNally. The free agent floodgates had opened.

Other issues arose. Owners wanted compensation from teams that signed their free agents. The players believed that would restrict their freedom. The result was a strike in 1981 that wiped out two months of the regular season. The two sides continued to squabble. The battle between players and owners became destructive in 1994. That is when their impasse resulted in a strike that began in August and destroyed the rest of the season. The playoffs and World Series were canceled. The players did not return to work until after the early part of the 1995 season was wiped out too. But labor peace has since reigned. There were no work stoppages from 1996 through 2019.

SOARING SALARIES

The revolution in baseball that brought freedom to players had an incredible effect on salaries. The annual minimum salary for major league players in 1967 was $6,000. It had reached only $16,000 around the advent of free agency in 1975. It continued to rise and reached $563,500 in 2020. The average annual player salary was $19,000 in 1967 and $44,676 in 1975. It soared to more than $4 million by 2018.[1]

THE SCANDALS OF BASEBALL

Sports in America have for generations attracted illegal gambling. Gamblers have tried to influence players to intentionally lose games so money can be made by betting on the other team. But it was not until 1919 that this kind of problem in baseball was exposed. That was the year of the Black Sox scandal.

Eight Chicago White Sox players took part in a scheme to throw the World Series to the Cincinnati Reds. The Sox were heavily favored to win the championship. But rumors persisted during the series that players had accepted bribes to lose on purpose, which they did. A grand jury investigation cleared the players despite two of them admitting to cheating. Kenesaw Mountain Landis, hired by the AL and NL owners as the league's commissioner to deal with the scandal, was not so forgiving. He banned all eight players from the sport for life. Included was legendary outfielder "Shoeless" Joe Jackson, who would have been a certain Hall of Famer had he not been involved.

Decades later, gambling prevented another surefire Hall of Fame inclusion. That was Pete Rose, who compiled a major league record 4,256 hits during his brilliant career, mostly with Cincinnati. Rose was investigated for—and later admitted to—gambling on baseball during his time as manager of the Reds. He was booted from the job and banished from baseball for life in 1989. Debates have raged

A statue of "Shoeless" Joe Jackson stands outside a minor league ballpark in South Carolina.

ever since over whether Rose should be reinstated and become eligible for the Hall of Fame. Supporters cite that he was never accused of wrongdoing during his incredible playing career.

MLB was forced to deal with another scandal 30 years later. That was when it was revealed that the Houston Astros cheated on the way to their 2017 World Series championship. Players that had been on that team spoke about an elaborate system that allowed the Astros to illegally steal signs from opposing catchers. Those signs were relayed to the Houston batters by banging on a garbage can near the dugout. This signaled whether the pitcher was about to throw a fastball or breaking ball. The result was that Astros hitters knew what pitches were coming. It's legal in baseball for a runner on second base to see a catcher's signals and convey them to the batter. But using other means to steal signals is against the rules.

MLB commissioner Rob Manfred suspended Houston general manager Jeff Luhnow and manager A. J. Hinch, both of whom were later fired by the team. Former Astros coach Alex Cora, who was hired as Boston's manager in 2018, also lost his job. And Carlos Beltran, an Astros player in 2017 who had been hired to manage the New York Mets in 2019, was fired before getting a chance to manage a game. But many fans complained that Houston hitters who benefited from the sign-stealing scheme should also have been suspended. And critics of the punishment suggested that the Astros should have been forced to give up their World Series crown.

Whether they involved gambling or on-field cheating, such scandals have given MLB a black eye. They force fans and even players to question whether games are being

MLB commissioner Rob Manfred spoke about the Astros scandal in February 2020 during a press conference at the spring training facility of the Atlanta Braves.

played honestly. The sport loses credibility if the outcomes of games have been altered by gambling or cheating.

THE STEROID ERA

Gambling and sign stealing have not been the only forms of cheating in baseball. It can be argued that another did even more damage to the integrity of the sport. This was the steroid scandal of the late 1990s and early 2000s.

What some believe was the most shameful period in the history of the sport began in 1998 as Mark McGwire and Sammy Sosa battled to break the single-season home run record. Reporters noticed in McGwire's locker a jar of androstenedione pills, often known as andros. This drug is meant to increase muscle size and strength. The revelation spurred fans to believe the incredible rise in home runs was not being achieved cleanly.

MLB implemented its first random drug testing policy in 2003. Three years later, after Barry Bonds had broken McGwire's home run record by slamming 73, grand jury testimony was leaked that indicated Bonds and other players had been using steroids to gain strength. Over the next several years many of the premier players in baseball were either accused of or proven to have been using steroids. Included were Bonds, McGwire, Sosa, and pitching standout Roger Clemens. Superstar sluggers such as Rafael Palmeiro, Alex Rodriguez, and Manny Ramirez

ALL ABOUT BONDS

The most controversial figure of the steroid era is Barry Bonds. The outfielder began his career with the Pittsburgh Pirates. The son of major league star Bobby Bonds, he won two NL MVP Awards before signing a lucrative multiyear free agent contract with San Francisco. He earned another MVP Award in his first season with the Giants and continued to thrive. Pitchers feared him to such an extent that they often simply issued intentional walks rather than throw him anything he could drive out of the park. Bonds led the league in walks 12 times and set an all-time major league record with 2,558 walks. He also shattered Hank Aaron's career home run mark by smashing 762. But he was roundly criticized for a perceived snobbish attitude and meanness toward the media, for which he apologized after his playing career. Evidence of steroid use to enhance his production continued to contribute to his unpopularity.

were suspended. Rodriguez, who had starred with the Texas Rangers and New York Yankees, told cable network ESPN he had used steroids to justify a $252 million contract.[2]

Players accused of steroid abuse were questioned by a government committee in March 2005. Bonds, McGwire, and Palmeiro denied ever using such substances. MLBPA executive director Donald Fehr stated that performance-enhancing drugs had no place in the game. "Playing major league baseball requires talent, drive, intelligence, determination, and grit," he said. "Steroids have no place in the equation."[3]

Drug testing later resulted in the suspensions of many players. This led to the end of the steroid era, which had tainted baseball forever. Players such as Bonds, McGwire, Sosa, Palmeiro, Rodriguez, Ramirez, and Clemens all boast career statistics easily worthy of Hall of Fame inclusion. But through 2019 none of them had been selected. Voters have consistently held accusations or proof of steroid use against them.

HOW THEY'RE PUNISHED

An MLB drug policy had been in effect since 1991. But it was rewritten in 2004 to include suspensions for those testing positive for performance-enhancing drugs (PEDs). The original policy included suspensions of ten days for

KEN
GRIFFEY JR.

Ken Griffey Jr.'s father played for the dominant Cincinnati Reds of the 1970s. Unlike many stars of his era, the younger Griffey was never accused of taking PEDs to boost performance. He certainly did not need any help. It can be argued that only injuries prevented Griffey from being mentioned alongside Willie Mays and Babe Ruth as the greatest all-around player in baseball history. Griffey, who played nearly his entire career with Seattle and Cincinnati, finished his career in 2010 with 630 home runs. His prowess as a hitter was matched by his brilliance as a center fielder. Griffey won a Gold Glove in ten consecutive seasons before injuries began taking a toll and prevented him from playing full seasons.

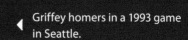

◄ Griffey homers in a 1993 game in Seattle.

first offenses, 30 days for second offenses, 60 days for third offenses, and one year for fourth offenses.[4]

The updated policy strengthened the ban on PEDs such as steroids. Government officials pressured MLB to implement penalties of 50 games and 100 games for first- and second-time offenders. A third offense would result in a lifetime ban from baseball. Penalties adopted in 2014 were even harsher. They included 80 games for first-time offenders, 162 games for second-time offenders, and a permanent ban for third-time offenders.[5] Players receiving the lifetime ban could apply for reinstatement to the commissioner of baseball after one year.

A DISTURBING PROBLEM FOR BASEBALL

Some major league players have been severely punished for their behavior off the field rather than for breaking the sport's rules. They have received suspensions for violence against others. Major League Baseball initiated a domestic violence policy in August 2015. It targeted players who assaulted girlfriends or family members such as wives and children. Twelve players received suspensions under the new policy from March 2016 through January 2020. Among them were premier Yankees pitchers Aroldis Chapman and Domingo German.

THE PLACES THEY HAVE PLAYED

Chicago's Wrigley Field is among the most historic and storied ballparks in MLB. ▸

Millions of baseball fans feel an emotional connection to the ballparks in which they have watched their favorite teams. Players feel a similar attachment to those in which they have competed.

Fans connect such venues with attending their first games as children and seeing the huge expanses of green grass in the outfield. They may remember witnessing an event such as the All-Star Game or World Series. Players link places in which they have performed with great personal and team achievements or friendships they forged with teammates.

Every park, past and present, has been unique. That makes them different than the venues in pro football, basketball, and soccer. The playing fields and surfaces of other sports feature identical measurements. They are uniform within the rules of their sports. Though distances from the mound to home plate and from base to base are the same, every baseball field is different. Distances from home plate to fences in all areas vary from park to park. Walls over which batters send home runs can be short or tall. They can jut out in center field or stand invitingly close for batters along the right field corner. Fans may sit close to the field, leaving little room for foul balls. Or they may be quite distant to give infielders plenty of room to snag pop-ups. The uniqueness of every venue is part of baseball's charm.

Fans have been streaming to Fenway Park to watch the Red Sox play for more than a century.

That is also why two franchises have refused to move. The Boston Red Sox and Chicago Cubs are so linked historically to their iconic parks that they have resisted all temptation to build bigger and more modern stadiums. Legendary Fenway Park has remained the home of the Sox since 1912. It features the Green Monster, the most famous and largest wall in baseball at 240 feet (73 m) wide and 37 feet (11 m) tall.[1] The Cubs have been playing since 1916 in Wrigley Field, which is best known for its ivy-covered walls.

Other ballparks have their own unique touches. Beyond the center field fence in Yankee Stadium is Monument Park, which features plaques of Babe Ruth, Lou Gehrig, Mickey Mantle, and other legends who have played for the most dominant club in baseball history. Fountains and a waterfall cascade down beyond the fence at Kauffman Stadium in Kansas City, home of the Royals. Fans can even take a dip in a swimming pool behind the right field fence at Chase Field, where the Arizona Diamondbacks play their home games.

HOW BALLPARKS HAVE EVOLVED

Early professional teams of the late 1800s and early 1900s played on baseball grounds with limited seating. Fans would often stand and crowd around the field to watch games. The growing popularity of baseball motivated clubs to build larger stadiums for their teams. The first were Shibe Park in Philadelphia and Forbes Field in Pittsburgh, both of which opened in 1909. Venues such as Fenway Park and Wrigley Field soon followed.

Other longtime homes for MLB teams were built later, including Ebbets Field in Brooklyn, Crosley Field in Cincinnati, Sportsman's Park in Saint Louis, Municipal Stadium in Cleveland, and Tiger Stadium in Detroit. The smaller ballparks of that era had charm and personality based on size and unique touches. For instance, the home run fence in Ebbets Field ranged from a mere 297 feet (91 m) away down the right field line to a massive 402 feet (123 m) in right-center field.[2]

Far less charm awaited many players and fans in the 1960s and early 1970s. Teams that shared homes with pro football teams moved into huge bowl-like domed or open-air stadiums. Among them were the Astrodome in Houston, Riverfront Stadium in Cincinnati, and Three Rivers Stadium in Pittsburgh. Many fans complained that they did not feel like ballparks but rather football venues with baseball diamonds painted on their fields.

A new era brought ballparks back full circle. Major league franchises of the 1990s and beyond began moving into smaller and more distinctive parks with stronger personalities. The first to break the mold was Oriole Park at Camden Yards in Baltimore. Others still occupied are Progressive Field in Cleveland, Coors Field in Denver, Oracle Park in San Francisco, Minute Maid Park in Houston, and Miller Park in Milwaukee. Among the features in many newer parks are stands nearer to the fields so fans can feel closer to the players, along with shorter distances between home plate and fences that result in more home runs.

Oakland Coliseum is among the stadiums that have been shared between baseball and football teams.

The evolution of ballparks reflects baseball history. It shows how MLB and its franchises have sought to attract fans in different eras of the sport. Teams seek to lure fans to pay to witness games in person rather than watch them on television for free. Newer ballparks have added bars and restaurants, and the stadium vendors offer a wider variety of food choices. Postgame fireworks often light up the sky. The goal of these amenities and features is to attract fans in ways that extend beyond the game itself.

A PEEK INTO THE FUTURE

Baseball was once proud of being known as America's pastime. But there is little doubt that football has passed it by as the most popular sport in the United States. It's also clear that many in the younger generations have not embraced baseball to the extent that their parents and grandparents did. MLB will continue to work on creating more interest, especially among younger people. It has begun to address issues that have brought criticism.

Among them is the pace of the game. Many fans believe games simply last too long, at an average of more than three hours. MLB has experimented with game clocks that limit the time between pitches. A new rule implemented in 2020 forces relief pitchers to face at least three batters before they can be replaced in the middle of an inning. That cuts down on the number of pitching changes, which drag out the length of games. Another possibility that has been discussed is placing a runner on second base to start

MLB AND COVID-19

In early 2020, a new disease called COVID-19 swept the globe, leaving millions infected and hundreds of thousands dead. To slow its spread, health officials instructed people to maintain physical distance between each other. This had a dramatic impact on MLB. On March 12, the league announced it was canceling preseason spring training games and delaying the season's opening by two weeks. Four days later, it said the season would not start until at least mid-May. In April, MLB officials discussed options for the season, including having all teams play at a few Arizona stadiums, with no fans present. However, the league said it did not have detailed plans for that alternative, adding that it was "not ready . . . to endorse any particular format for staging games in light of the rapidly changing public health situation."[3] COVID-19 paralyzed MLB and sports leagues worldwide.

extra innings in an attempt to add excitement and finish games faster.

MLB is also exploring ways to create more action. The alarming increase in strikeouts has resulted in fewer balls put into play. But that is not likely to change until more players stop swinging for the fences. There is little that league officials can do to prevent that from happening aside from forcing clubs to move fences back and using balls that do not travel as far. But MLB also knows that its fans love to see home runs.

Meanwhile, the field of analytics has motivated defenses to use dramatic shifts against hitters by placing three players on one side of the infield against hitters they suspect will hit the ball in that direction. Many supporters state that batters must become more versatile and hit the ball away from the shifts. But MLB has looked into banning the shift and ensuring that two fielders are positioned on each side of the infield.

Only time will tell how MLB will deal with its myriad issues. Millions of fans will continue to embrace the sport they love no matter what is done in the name of improvement. But one can only speculate as to what baseball will look like in the future. And only time will tell whether its overall popularity rises or falls.

ALL-TIME LEADERS

HITS

1. Pete ROSE
2. Ty COBB
3. Hank AARON
4. Stan MUSIAL
5. Tris SPEAKER

HOME RUNS

1. Barry BONDS
2. Hank AARON
3. Babe RUTH
4. Alex RODRIGUEZ
5. Willie MAYS

STRIKEOUTS

1. Nolan RYAN
2. Randy JOHNSON
3. Roger CLEMENS
4. Steve CARLTON
5. Burt BLYLEVEN

PITCHING WINS

1. Cy YOUNG
2. Walter JOHNSON
3. Pete ALEXANDER (tied)
3. Christy MATHEWSON (tied)
5. Pud GALVIN

ESSENTIAL FACTS

Significant Events

o The 1869 Cincinnati Red Stockings became the first all-professional baseball team and won all 64 games they played.

o The American League was formed in 1901 and joined the National League to create the current structure of Major League Baseball.

o Slugger Babe Ruth was sold from the Boston Red Sox to the New York Yankees before the 1920 season, setting off a home run revolution in baseball and a Yankees dynasty.

o The Brooklyn Dodgers signed Jackie Robinson in 1946, ending a shameful period of segregation in baseball and opening up the door for full-scale integration.

o The Red Sox ended the Curse of the Bambino in 2004 by beating the Yankees in the playoffs and Saint Louis Cardinals in the World Series for their first crown in 86 years.

Key Players

o Detroit Tigers outfielder Ty Cobb was both one of the greatest—and most unpleasant—players of all time. His .366 career batting average remains the best ever compiled.

o Pitcher Cy Young racked up an incredible 511 major league victories, far more than any other hurler in baseball history. It is a record that almost certainly will remain unbroken.

o Boston outfielder Ted Williams is considered by many the greatest hitter ever.

o Giants superstar Willie Mays was arguably the greatest all-around player in baseball history. He hit for average and for power, stole bases, and was a sensational defensive center fielder.

- Angels outfielder Mike Trout has been the most dominant player of the 2000s. He won three AL MVP Awards and finished second four other times in his first eight seasons.

Key Teams

- The New York Yankees were easily the most dominant franchise in baseball over the years. They won 27 World Series championships, including 16 from 1936 to 1962.

- The Los Angeles Dodgers moved from Brooklyn in 1958 and emerged as a force in the National League.

- The Boston Red Sox became the most successful team of the new century. They won World Series crowns in 2004, 2007, 2013, and 2018.

- The Saint Louis Cardinals have captured more National League crowns than any team and have arguably the most loyal fan base in baseball.

Quote

"The Giants win the pennant! The Giants win the pennant! The Giants win the pennant! . . . And they're going crazy!"

—Radio announcer Russ Hodges in the most famous call in baseball history, made after "The Shot Heard 'Round the World" in the 1951 National League championship

GLOSSARY

ace
The top starting pitcher on a team.

androstenedione
A steroid used to increase testosterone and build strength.

closer
The relief pitcher on a team used to close out victories.

collective bargaining agreement
A negotiated contract between employees and higher-ranking management, usually regarding working conditions or pay.

draft
A process in which sports teams select the top eligible players to join them.

dynasty
An extended period of excellence or success for a team.

free agency
The state of being allowed to sell one's services to anyone in the market.

impasse
A point in negotiations in which neither side sees room for compromise.

integration
Acceptance of people belonging to different groups (such as races) as equals in society.

interleague
In baseball, describing games played between National League and American League teams.

journeyman
A reliable but not necessarily outstanding player or coach.

parity
In sports leagues, a situation in which no team dominates and many are close in level of success on the field.

pennant

An American League or National League championship.

perfect game

A pitching performance in which no batter reaches base.

pinch hitter

A hitter that replaces another hitter in the lineup during the course of a game.

pitching win

A statistic awarded when a pitcher pitches at least five innings and his team goes on to win the game.

rivalry

Heated competition between two parties over a long period.

roster

The total list of players on a particular team.

segregated

Separated based on race, gender, ethnicity, or other factors.

stolen base

A base reached by a runner without the ball being hit by the batter.

union

An organized association of workers, often in a trade or profession, formed to protect and further their rights and interests.

ADDITIONAL RESOURCES

Selected Bibliography

Kepner, Tyler. *K: A History of Baseball in Ten Pitches*. Doubleday, 2019.

"Major League Baseball Records." *Baseball Almanac*, n.d., baseball-almanac.com. Accessed 1 Mar. 2020.

"MLB World Series Winners." *ESPN*, n.d., espn.com. Accessed 1 Mar. 2020.

Further Readings

Allen, John. *The Science and Technology of Baseball*. ReferencePoint, 2020.

Harris, Duchess, JD, PhD, with Carla Mooney. *Fighting Stereotypes in Sports*. Abdo, 2019.

Sandalow, Brian. *Jose Altuve: Baseball Superstar*. Abdo, 2020.

Online Resources

To learn more about MLB, please visit **abdobooklinks.com** or scan this QR code. These links are routinely monitored and updated to provide the most current information available.

More Information

For more information on this subject, contact or visit the following organizations:

National Baseball Hall of Fame and Museum

25 Main St.
Cooperstown, NY 13326
888-425-5633
baseballhall.org

The National Baseball Hall of Fame and Museum has exhibits that feature all the inducted players, managers, and others who have proven their baseball greatness, as well as the famous events in the history of the sport.

Negro Leagues Baseball Museum

1616 E. Eighteenth St.
Kansas City, MO 64108
816-221-1920
nlbm.com

The Negro Leagues Baseball Museum allows visitors to relive the many years in which African American players were shunned from Major League Baseball and forged competition of their own. Visitors can celebrate the lives and careers of such immortals as Satchel Paige, "Cool Papa" Bell, Josh Gibson, and Oscar Charleston.

SOURCE NOTES

CHAPTER 1. THE SHOT HEARD 'ROUND THE WORLD

1. "The Shot Heard 'Round the World." *YouTube*, uploaded by Jim Murphy, 7 Apr. 2007, youtube.com. Accessed 27 Mar. 2020.

CHAPTER 2. DEAD BALL, LIVE BALL, AND THE SULTAN OF SWAT

1. Matt Rothenberg. "150 Years Ago, Pro Baseball Began in Cincinnati." *Baseball Hall of Fame*, n.d., baseballhall.org. Accessed 27 Mar. 2020.

2. "Home Run Baker." *Baseball Reference*, n.d., baseball-reference.com. Accessed 27 Mar. 2020.

3. "Top 10 Chicago All-Star Game Moments." *Chicago Tribune*, n.d., chicagotribune.com. Accessed 27 Mar. 2020.

4. Daniel Wyatt. "Wyatt: Remembering the Gashouse Gang." *National Pastime Museum*, 16 Feb. 2015, sabr.org. Accessed 27 Mar. 2020.

CHAPTER 3. FROM THE FORTIES TO FREE AGENCY

1. "Major League Baseball Miscellaneous Year-by-Year Averages and Totals." *Baseball Reference*, n.d., baseball-reference.com. Accessed 27 Mar. 2020.

2. Dave Anderson. "Jackie Robinson, First Black in Major League, Dies." *New York Times*, 25 Oct. 1972, nytimes.com. Accessed 27 Mar. 2020.

3. Rhiannon Walker. "Willie Mays Comes Down with 'The Catch.'" *The Undefeated*, 28 Sept. 2016, theundefeated.com. Accessed 27 Mar. 2020.

4. "Minimum Salary." *Baseball Reference*, n.d., baseball-reference.com. Accessed 27 Mar. 2020.

5. "Minimum Salary."

CHAPTER 4. CREATING THE MODERN GAME

None.

CHAPTER 5. DOWN ON THE FARM

1. Christina Gough. "Average Player Salary in Major League Baseball from 2003 to 2019." *Statista*, 9 Aug. 2019, statista.com. Accessed 27 Mar. 2020.

2. "2019 MLB Attendance & Team Age." *Baseball Reference*, n.d., baseball-reference.com. Accessed 27 Mar. 2020.

3. Ian Gordon. "Minor League Baseball Players Make Poverty-Level Wages." *Mother Jones*, July/Aug. 2014, motherjones.com. Accessed 27 Mar. 2020.

4. "Minor League Baseball Timeline." *MiLB*, n.d., milb.com. Accessed 27 Mar. 2020.

5. Jesse Goldberg-Strassler. "The Last Great MiLB Contraction." *Ballpark Digest*, 5 Dec. 2019, ballparkdigest.com. Accessed 27 Mar. 2020.

6. "Minor League Baseball Posts Attendance Increase of over One Million Fans in 2019." *MiLB*, 10 Sept. 2019, milb.com. Accessed 27 Mar. 2020.

CHAPTER 6. RIVALRIES AND AWARDS

1. "1949 Boston Red Sox Schedule." *Baseball Reference*, n.d., baseball-reference.com. Accessed 27 Mar. 2020.

2. Glenn Liebman. "5 Great Quotes about Yankees-Red Sox Rivalry." *ESPN*, n.d., espn.com. Accessed 27 Mar. 2020.

3. Tim Keown. "When the Earth Moved the Series." *ESPN*, 17 Oct. 2014, espn.com. Accessed 27 Mar. 2020.

CHAPTER 7. THE SEASON STRUCTURE

1. Wells Dusenbury. "MLB Worst: Marlins' Low Attendance Hit Bottom Monday Night." *South Florida Sun Sentinel*, 27 Aug. 2019, sun-sentinel.com. Accessed 27 Mar. 2020.

2. Dieter Kurtenbach. "Ranking the Best Baseball Towns in (North) America." *Fox Sports*, 9 May 2017, foxsports.com. Accessed 27 Mar. 2020.

CHAPTER 8. STRIKES, SCANDALS, AND STEROIDS

1. "Minimum Salary." *Baseball Reference*, n.d., baseball-reference.com. Accessed 27 Mar. 2020.

2. "MLB Doping Timeline." *Reuters*, 5 Aug. 2013, reuters.com. Accessed 27 Mar. 2020.

3. "Notable Quotes: Steroid Hearings." *Fox News*, 17 Mar. 2005, foxnews.com. Accessed 27 Mar. 2020.

4. "A Timeline of MLB's Drug-Testing Rules." *USA Today*, 28 Mar. 2014, usatoday.com. Accessed 27 Mar. 2020.

5. Bob Nightengale. "MLB Toughens Drug Agreement Provisions." *USA Today*, 28 Mar. 2014, usatoday.com. Accessed 27 Mar. 2020.

CHAPTER 9. THE PLACES THEY HAVE PLAYED

1. Brian Viner. "Baseball: Fenway—More than Just a Park." *Independent*, 19 Apr. 2012, independent.co.uk. Accessed 27 Mar. 2020.

2. "The History of Ebbets Field." *Baseball Almanac*, n.d., baseball-almanac.com. Accessed 27 Mar. 2020.

3. Dayn Perry. "MLB's Plan to Have 30 Teams in Arizona Might Be Most Viable Path to 2020 Season, Report Says." *CBS Sports*, 13 Apr. 2020, cbssports.com. Accessed 28 Apr. 2020.

INDEX

Marty Gitlin

Marty Gitlin is a freelance sports book author based in Cleveland. He has had more than 150 books published, including many about baseball. Martin won more than 45 awards as a sports journalist, including first place from the Associated Press for his coverage of the 1995 World Series. That organization also selected him as one of the top four feature writers in Ohio.